Celebrate!

India

Robyn Hardyman

W
FRANKLIN WATTS
LONDON • SYDNEY

This edition first published in 2009
by Franklin Watts

Copyright © 2009
The Brown Reference Group Ltd

Franklin Watts
338 Euston Road
London NW1 3BH

Franklin Watts Australia
Level 17/207 Kent Street
Sydney, NSW 2000

A CIP catalogue record for this book is available
from the British Library.
Dewey no: 915.4

ISBN 978 0 7496 8422 8

Printed in China

Franklin Watts is a division of Hachette Children's Books,
an Hachette UK company.
www.hachette.co.uk

Note to parents and teachers concerning websites:
In the book every effort has been made by the Publishers
to ensure that websites are suitable for children, that
they are of the highest educational value, and that they
contain no inappropriate or offensive material. However,
because of the nature of the Internet, it is impossible to
guarantee that the contents of these sites will not be
altered. We advise that Internet access is supervised by
a responsible adult.

For The Brown Reference Group Ltd
Project Editor: Sarah Eason
Designer: Paul Myerscough
Picture Researcher: Maria Joannou
Indexer: Claire Throp
Design Manager: David Poole
Managing Editor: Miranda Smith
Editorial Director: Lindsey Lowe

Consultant Editor
Peter Lewis
Writer and Editor for the American Geographical
Society, New York

Author
Robyn Hardyman

Contents

Welcome to India

India is a large country in southern Asia. It is the second most populated country in the world. In its long history, India has been part of many great empires.

Today India is an independent country and a **democracy**. India's **economy** is growing fast and some areas of the country are very prosperous. However, many millions of people still live in **poverty**.

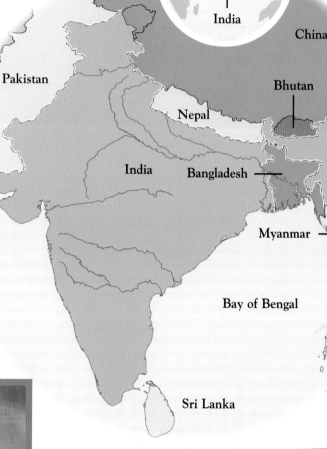

India

China

Pakistan

Nepal

Bhutan

India

Bangladesh

Myanmar

Bay of Bengal

Sri Lanka

Taj Mahal

The Taj Mahal is one of the most beautiful buildings in the world. It was built between 1631 and 1653 by the Mughal emperor Shah Jahan, in memory of his wife. It is made entirely of marble and covered with semi-precious stones.

Indian borders

India together with its neighbouring countries Pakistan, Bangladesh and Sri Lanka are known as the **Indian subcontinent**. India also includes more than 300 islands in the Arabian Sea, Bay of Bengal and Indian Ocean. It shares land borders with Pakistan, China, Nepal, Bhutan, Bangladesh and Myanmar (Burma). India has a long coastline, washed by the Indian Ocean, the Arabian Sea and the Bay of Bengal.

INDIAN FACTS

FULL NAME	*Republic of India*
CAPITAL CITY	*New Delhi*
AREA	*3,289,285 square km*
POPULATION IN 2008	*1,120,000,000*
MAIN LANGUAGES	*Hindi, English, and at least 16 others*
MAIN RELIGIONS	*Hinduism, Islam, Christianity, Sikhism, Buddhism, Jainism*
CURRENCY	*Rupee*

Emblem of India

These lions are India's official **emblem**. The Indian King Asoka, who ruled in the third century B.C.E, had them carved at the top of the stone pillars on which his laws were written. The wheel at the lions' feet appears on the Indian flag.

Indian religions

More than 80 per cent of Indian people practise Hinduism, a religion with many gods and goddesses (such as the god Shiva, right). People who practise Islam are called Muslims. They believe in one God, Allah. Sikhs believe that they should work hard to serve others. Buddhists do not believe in one God, but believe in kharma – if we perform good deeds on Earth we will eventually go to Heaven. Jainism is an ancient Indian religion that teaches non-violence and compassion.

History Highlights

Over five thousand years, many different cultures have played a role in developing Indian society.

India is one of the oldest civilizations in the world – the first few cities grew up along the Indus River Valley from about 3,500 B.C.E. The first civilization included well-planned cities such as Lothal (right). The rulers were priests, called the Dravidians, who practised an early form of Hinduism. In about 1,500 B.C.E., the Aryan people of central Asia invaded from the north. They developed the **Sanskrit** language and the **caste** system (see box below).

WEB LINKS
Find out more about India's history at:
www.ancientindia.co.uk/index.html

The caste system
The Indian caste system is a rigid system of social groups, which still operates in India today. A person cannot change the caste into which they are born. The four main castes are called brahman, kshatria, vaisia and sudra. The lowest class of all is called untouchables. People within this caste are often only allowed to perform low-paid jobs and are not allowed to mix with people from higher castes.

Mongol invasion

In the thirteenth century, India was invaded from the north by Muslims called Mongols. In the sixteenth century, Babur, a descendant of the great Mongols Genghis Khan and Timur (Tamburlaine), invaded. He established the beginning of the great Mughal Empire. The Mughal dynasty ruled for over three hundred years, until 1857.

Hampi

The city of Hampi was the capital of the great Hindu kingdom of Vijayanagara in southern India. This kingdom lasted from 1336 to 1565.

Akbar (1556–1605)

Akbar was the grandson of Babur and the most popular of the Mughal emperors. He came to power when he was 13 years old. During his reign he strengthened the empire and formed his own religion. He was a great supporter of the arts. The main form of painting at that time was the **illuminated manuscript**. Akbar ordered many illuminated manuscripts, like the one on the left, and built a huge library of historical, classical Persian literature, as well as translations of Sanskrit texts.

Foreign rule

The Portuguese were the first Europeans to settle in India. They set up a factory in Goa in the fifteenth century and took control of the trade in spices and silks. The French and the British then arrived to compete with Portugal for this trade. In the eighteenth century, the British East India Company drove their French rivals out of the state of Bengal, and by the nineteenth century, the British controlled most of the country. In 1877, Queen Victoria (left) took the title Empress of India. Britain ruled India until 1947. In 1885, the Indian National Congress was set up by Indians who wanted more of a say in their country's government. When the British rejected their demands, a movement for independence began. From 1919, the leader of this movement was Mohandas Gandhi.

Gandhi (1869-1948)

Mohandas Gandhi led the Indian people in their struggle for independence from British rule. He was known as 'Mahatma', meaning 'great soul'. As leader of the Indian National Congress Party, he led a series of peaceful protests against British rule and was arrested many times. Gandhi wanted to unite the Hindus and Muslims who were fighting each other in India. He was killed in 1948 by a Hindu who could not accept his message of peace. He has been featured on the Indian rupee banknotes since 1996.

Red Fort

The Red Fort in Delhi was built by the Mughal emperor Shah Jahan in 1639 as the palace for his new capital, Shahjahanabad. The British army once occupied this building. It is now a symbol of India's independence, and on Independence Day the **prime minister** speaks to the nation from here.

DID YOU KNOW?
India gained its independence from Britain in 1947, and the separate Muslim state of Pakistan (which initially included present-day Bangladesh) was created.

Fighting for Kashmir

During the separation of Pakistan from India many people were killed. There have been three wars between India and Pakistan since 1947, two of them over the territory of Kashmir.

Growing economy

This is India's Stock Exchange in Mumbai. Mumbai (Bombay) is the financial capital of India. Since the 1980s, India's economy has been growing fast. Millions of Indians still live in poverty. However, some people predict that during the twenty-first century, India will once again become one of the wealthiest countries in the world.

Fly the Flag

India's national flag was designed in 1947, when the country gained independence from Britain. The flag is known as the Tiranga and is a symbol of freedom throughout India.

The Indian flag has three horizontal bars of equal width. The orange (**saffron**) bar represents courage and sacrifice. Truth and purity are represented by the white bar. The green represents faith and growth. The wheel in the middle is called the Asoka Chakra, or wheel of law. It is also a symbol of the circle of life, death and rebirth.

Indian star

The Star of India was the coat of arms of British India. It was shown on flags used for all official ceremonies, until it was replaced with the Tiranga flag.

Flag of justice

The Asoka Chakra is named after the Mauryan King Asoka (see page 5). It has twenty-four spokes, one for each hour of the day, to symbolize justice.

DID YOU KNOW?

Rangoli designs are sometimes drawn on the floor of a house, near the front door, to welcome guests. The word *rangoli* is made up of two words joined together, *rang* and *avalli*. *Rangoli* means 'row of colours'.

Flag of freedom

The late Indian prime minister Pandit Nehru (1889-1964), right, described the Tiranga as a symbol of freedom not only for India, but for all humankind.

 ## Try this!

Make greetings cards with rangoli *designs*

- A rangoli *is a colourful design made on the floor near the entrance to a house, to welcome guests. The designs are found across India. They can be square, rectangular or circular, and are often* **symmetrical**. *Some designs are hundreds of years old. They are handed down from mother to daughter.*

- *Take two pieces of card, 210 x 297 mm in size. Fold each piece in half to make a greetings card.*

- *Draw a square of dots on the first card. The dots should be evenly spaced within the square.*

- *Starting at the top of the square, draw lines between the dots to make a pattern, like the ones opposite.*

- *Now colour in your design using bright colours.*

For your second card, look at these designs for ideas!

Hymn to India

Jana Gana Mana is the national anthem of India. It is the first of five verses of a poem written in Bengali by the famous Indian poet Rabindranath Tagore. The music was also written by Tagore.

The **national anthem** was first sung at the Indian National Congress in 1911. In 1919, Tagore translated the anthem into English for the first time. *Jana Gana Mana* was officially adopted as the Indian national anthem in 1950.

O! Dispenser of India's destiny, you are the ruler of the minds of all people
Your name rouses the hearts of Punjab, Sindh, Gujarat, the Maratha country, in the Dravida country, Utkala and Bengal;
It echoes in the hills of the Vindhyas and Himalayas, it mingles in the rhapsodies of the pure waters of Yamuna and the Ganges.
They chant only your name.
They seek only your auspicious blessings.
They sing only the glory of your victory.
The salvation of all people waits in your hands,
O! Dispenser of India's destiny, you are the ruler of the minds of all people
Victory to you, Victory to you,
Victory, Victory, Victory, Victory to you!

Rabindranath Tagore

Rabindranath Tagore wrote plays and novels as well as poems. In 1913, he won the Nobel Prize for Literature. The English translation of the anthem is shown above.

National song

India also has a national song, *Vande Mataram*. It was composed in 1876 by Bankimchandra Chattopadhyay. It celebrates India, and was a cry for India to be free from British rule. *Vande Mataram* is sung every day in many schools across India. It is not popular with some Muslims because it praises a Hindu goddess, Durga (right).

DID YOU KNOW?
It takes about 52 seconds to sing the full version of *Jana Gana Mana*. A shortened version takes just 20 seconds to sing.

Celebration song

This picture shows school children during the **centenary** celebrations for *Vande Mataram*, in 2006. On 7th September, children across India sang the national song at the same time.

Regions of India

India is an enormous and beautiful country with many different kinds of landscape. These include mountains, deserts, tropical rainforests, fertile plains and a dry plateau.

In the north the mighty Himalaya mountains separate India from China and Nepal. Some of the world's highest mountains are found here. Large rivers such as the Ganges and the Brahmaputra flow down from the mountains to India's northern plains. In the northwest is the Thar desert. In the south is an enormous **plateau**, called the Deccan. Along the western coast run the Western Ghats mountains.

Himalayan wilderness

The Nanda Devi National Park and the Valley of Flowers National Park form one of the most spectacular wilderness areas in the Himalayas. Mount Nanda Devi, over 8,530 metres high, towers above the Nanda Devi National Park.

Farming and fishing

The plains contain the most fertile land in India, where wheat is grown. In the south rice is the biggest crop. India's long coastline supports a large fishing industry. Fishermen catch fish to sell both at home and abroad.

River Ganges

Hindus believe the Ganges is a **sacred** river, and that bathing in it can wash away their sins.

Climate

India's climate is very varied. Its snow-covered mountains are very cold, but its plains and rainforests can be extremely hot. India's monsoon season begins in the south in June, and covers the whole country by the end of the month. It lasts until September. The monsoon season brings heavy rain. The monsoon provides much-needed water to crops such as tea (below).

Where do Indians live?

Three-quarters of people in India live in the countryside and work on the land. However, many millions of people live in the cities. Delhi, Mumbai and Calcutta all have populations of over 10 million. The cities are overcrowded and living conditions are often poor.

What's Cooking?

The food Indian people eat is often influenced by their religion. Many Hindus are strict vegetarians, because of their respect for animal life. However, some eat fish and chicken. Muslims do not eat any pig products because they are forbidden to by their holy book, the Qu'ran.

As in regional cooking around the world, recipes in India depend on what is grown, caught or otherwise available locally. Rice, millet and bread are staple foods. Food is flavoured with herbs and spices such as chilli, coriander, ginger and turmeric.

DID YOU KNOW?
Saffron (called *kesar* in India) is a spice that comes from the inside of crocus flowers. It is the most expensive spice in the world. It takes 165,000 crocus flowers to produce just 1 kilogram of saffron.

Savoury snacks
On the streets of towns and cities all over India you will find stalls selling savoury snacks called *chaat*.

A sweet tooth

Puddings are always eaten at Indian festivals and holidays. They are made with milk, sugar, nuts and fruits.

Samosa

This deep-fried pastry is filled with vegetables and is one of the types of *chaat* sold all over India.

What's on the menu?

Indian dishes are usually served in large bowls. A typical meal is shown below.

dhal
a dish of lentils and spices

palak paneer
a vegetable curry dish made of spinach and cheese

raita
a plain yoghurt, sometimes mixed with cucumber, mint or coriander leaves

chapatis
a round, flat bread

Try this!

Let's make cardamom scented rice pudding

Ingredients:
1 litre milk
60 g long grain Basmati rice
25 g sugar
4 cardamom pods, crushed
5 g pistachio nuts, sliced
5 g raisins
a few strands of saffron soaked in a little milk

Soak the rice in water for about 30 minutes. In a large bowl grind it using a little of the soaking water, to make a fine paste. Bring the milk to the boil in a large saucepan and let it simmer. Pour a little of it into the bowl of rice paste and stir well. Add the contents of the bowl to the saucepan and cook over a low heat for 12 minutes, or until it thickens. Stir in the sugar and cook for an additional 4 minutes. Remove from the heat and stir in the raisins and saffron, then sprinkle the cardamom powder on top. Garnish with sliced pistachios. Serve chilled.

How Do I Say...?

India has more languages than any other country – fifteen main languages and hundreds of other languages and dialects. The most widespread language is Hindi, which is spoken by about one in five of the population – mostly those living in the north. The other official language is English. Main languages include Bengali, Urdu, Punjabi, Gujarati, Tamil and Telegu.

The most popular form of greeting in India, especially when meeting elders, is to say *namaste* with your hands joined at chest level (right). This is also used when saying goodbye.

Words and phrases

English	Hindi	How to say it
hello/goodbye	namaste	nah-muh-stay
my name is	mera nam hai	meh-rah nahm hay
how are you?	ap kese hoi?	ahp kay-say ho
see you later	phir milengai	fihrr mee-len-ghay

DID YOU KNOW?
Indians prostrate before their parents, elders and teachers. This means they lie down before them and put their palms together in front of the other person's feet.

A country of many languages

In the busy city streets you may hear many different languages being spoken. Gujarati is spoken by about 46 million people in India, mostly in the state of Gujarat in the west of the country. There are many different Gujarati **dialects**. Bengali is spoken in the state of Bengal in north-east India. Urdu is spoken in India by about 48 million people, in places where there are large numbers of Muslims. Urdu is written from right to left, like Arabic and Persian. Urdu has 39 basic letters and 13 extra characters.

Seven Sisters

The seven states of northeast India are known as the Seven Sisters. Most of the people who live here are from small tribes

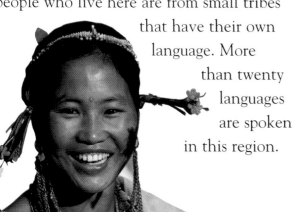

that have their own language. More than twenty languages are spoken in this region.

Indian saying

Haathi gaddhe mein girrta hai toh chuha bhi laat maarta hai. 'If an elephant falls in a ditch, then even a mouse will beat him.' This means that, when a powerful figure is in trouble, even the smallest and weakest will attack him.

Stories and Legends

Over 80 per cent of people in India are Hindu, and the Hindu religion has many wonderful stories about its gods and goddesses.

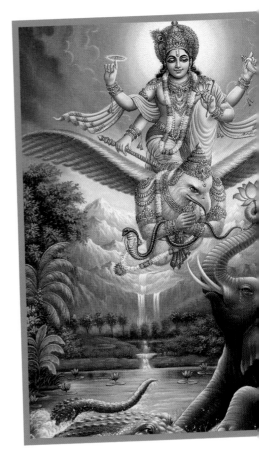

Hindus believe there are many more worlds and universes than there are drops of water in the holy River Ganges. They tell how Vishnu ordered Brahma (right) to create the first universe. Brahma was sitting on a lotus flower. He split the flower into three: he stretched one part into the heavens, he made another part into the Earth, and with the third part of the flower he created the skies. Worlds are looked after by Vishnu and destroyed by Shiva. These three gods are all part of the Supreme One.

The Mahabharata

The Mahabharata is an ancient story from India. This Hindu epic is one of the longest poems in the world, with more than 74,000 verses and about 1.8 million words. The main plot follows the lives of the five Pandava brothers, and is filled with monsters, gods and dragons. This painting of the tale (left) was commissioned by the Mughal Emperor Akbar.

The Ramayana

This epic poem tells the story of Rama, who is sent into exile by his father King Dashratha. Rama travels through the forests of India with his wife, Sita, who is kidnapped by Ravana, a demon king. Rama defeats the demon king with the help of an army of monkeys, returns home and is crowned king.

Shiva and Parvati

In Hindu legend, Shiva came to earth to marry Meenakshi, an incarnation of his partner, the goddess Parvati. Parvati had earlier descended to Earth as a child. When she grew up she ruled the city of Madurai. Shiva appeared on Earth and proposed to her. Meenakshi's brother, Vishnu, was travelling to conduct the marriage, but was tricked and delayed by another god, Indra. The marriage was then conducted by a local god. Angry Vishnu swore never to enter the city of Madurai, but later forgave his sister, and blessed her and Shiva.

The elephant god Ganesh

Ganesh, one of the most popular Hindu gods, is the son of Shiva and Parvati. He is said to have written the Mahabharata. He is shown with an elephant's head on a human body. One version of the story is that Ganesh was born with a human head, but Shiva beheaded him when he came between Shiva and his wife Parvati. Shiva then replaced Ganesh's head with that of an elephant. Ganesh is known as the Remover of Obstacles, and is prayed to particularly when people are beginning something new.

Art and Culture

India's cultural history is as diverse as its people. The traditional art of India is heavily influenced by religion.

India's long history has produced some truly beautiful buildings from many different cultures. There are wonderful Buddhist temples, such as the Dhamekh Stupa at Sarnath, Hindu temples such as the Sun Temple at Konark, and Muslim mosques such as the Jama Masjid in Delhi.

Golden Temple

Amritsar is in northwest India, in the state of Punjab. It is the site of the Harimandir Sahib, also known as the Golden Temple, the holiest place in the world for the Sikh religion. The Golden Temple was completed in 1604. The upper story is plated with gold and topped with a dome.

Indian dance

Classical Indian dancing was traditionally **part of religious ritual**. Dancers tell the stories of the Ramayana and the Mahabharata. There is great meaning in the dancers' gestures and movements, and their costumes and make-up are spectacular.

Pandit Ravi Shankar (born 1920)

Ravi Shankar is one of India's best-known musicians. He plays the sitar, a traditional Indian instrument with a long neck and up to 20 metal strings. He also composes classical music. When Shankar played with the Beatles in the 1960s, his music became popular all over the world. He still lives in India.

Bollywood

This picture is from the Indian film *Kabhi Kushi Kabhi Gham* (2001). India's multi-million-dollar film industry, known as Bollywood, is the biggest in the world. More than 800 films are made each year, most of them in Mumbai. They are the most widely watched films in the world, and the Indian film stars are treated like royalty. Bollywood films may be dramas, romances or comedies, but they always include lots of singing and dancing.

Handicrafts

India's villagers have a long history of creating beautiful craft objects, including metalwork, pottery and textiles, such as silk, for saris. A sari (left) is a traditional garment worn by Indian women. The 2,000-year-old tradition of making saris involves detailed work on the silk yarn, and each sari takes at least six months to make.

WEB LINKS
For more information about handicrafts in India go to:
www.kolkata.org.uk/culture/arts-crafts/handicrafts.html

Make Your Own Indian Mirror

Make a colourful Indian mirror to hang on your bedroom wall.

1 Cut a square the same size as the mirror tile out of the pink cardboard. To make the inside edge of the frame, draw a curved and pointed Indian arch on to the card. Make it as symmetrical as possible.

2 Carefully cut out the middle of the card, leaving the finished frame.

3 Stick strips of double-sided tape to the back of the frame. Do not remove the backing tape.

4 Turn the frame over. Dilute some PVA glue to make it easier to apply, and paint it over the front of the frame. Leave a narrow border around the edge.

5 Draw an elephant on the gold paper and cut it out. Stick it to the frame. If you don't want to use an elephant design, try a peacock or lotus pattern instead.

Protected peacocks

The peacock is India's national bird. Peacocks live wild in the forests, and hunting them is banned by law.

DID YOU KNOW?
The sacred lotus flower
is India's national flower.
It appears in many legends
and religious stories, and
in many Indian designs.
The flower is a symbol
of a pure heart and mind.

6 Sprinkle glitter all over the frame while the glue is still wet. Shake off any excess.

7 Peel off the backing on the double-sided tape and stick the frame on to the tile.

8 Decorate the frame with glitter and shiny and colourful stickers.

9 Glue a loop of string to the back of the tile, so that you can hang it up when it is dry.

Sports and Leisure

Indians in cities like to spend their free time going to the cinema, watching or playing sport, going out to restaurants or visiting friends and family at home. In the countryside cricket is also popular, but workers in the fields do not have much time for leisure.

The most popular sport in India is cricket. It was introduced to India by the British and it is played everywhere, from small villages to big cities. The Indian national cricket team is one of the best in the world, and millions of Indians watch it on television when it is competing. Many Indians also play hockey, which is India's national game. India's national hockey team has also been successful in international competitions.

Camel racing

In Rajastan the sport of camel racing is popular. Every year in November, thousands of people gather at the Pushkar Fair to watch the camels race.

Family life

Indian families can be large, with several generations living together. It is common for couples to live with their parents even after they are married and have children of their own. Indian families spend much of their time off just relaxing together.

Sachin Tendulkar (born 1973)

Sachin Tendulkar is India's biggest cricket star and one of the best batsmen in the world. He joined the national team at the age of sixteen and has scored more than 20,000 runs for India.

DID YOU KNOW?

Groups of Indian men often gather in the street to play *carrom*. This game is played with small flat discs on a square board with a pocket at each corner. Bigger discs are used to flick the smaller ones into the pockets.

Going to the cinema

Cinemas are everywhere in India's towns and cities, and going to see a film is the number one pastime. The Raj Mandir Cinema opened in 1976 and is the best-known cinema building in India.

Festivals and Holidays

More festivals are celebrated in India than anywhere else in the world. A festival may be held to welcome the seasons of the year, the harvest, the rains or the full moon. Others celebrate religious occasions, the birthdays of divine beings and saints, or the start of the New Year.

Diwali

In October or November Diwali, the Hindu festival of light, celebrates gods and mythical heroes. At Diwali, people decorate their houses with lamps and candles to welcome Lakshmi, the goddess of wealth. Fireworks are set off to scare away any evil spirits.

DID YOU KNOW?
Maha Kumbh Mela is India's biggest religious festival. It takes place only every twelve years, at the place where the Ganges and Yamuna rivers meet. In 2001, 70 million Hindus gathered there over a period of a month to bathe in the waters.

WEB LINKS
To find out more about Diwali go to:
www.diwalifestival.org

Muslim festival

Eid-el-Fitr is the main Muslim festival. It is celebrated in autumn after the month-long **fast** of Ramadan. During the fast, Muslims are not allowed to eat between sunrise and sunset. At Eid-el-Fitr, Muslims go to the mosque to give thanks for their blessings, and they meet their family for a large meal. One of the special Eid dishes in India is *savayya*, a dish of fine, toasted noodles. This is often served for the first breakfast after the fast.

Rama's victory

In northern India, people celebrate the Dussehra festival. This ten-day event celebrates the victory of the god Rama over the ten-headed demon king Ravana. On the last day, huge models of Ravana (below) and his brothers are set on fire.

Colourful festival

In February or March, Holi, the Hindu festival of *colour*, marks the end of winter. People throw coloured water and powder over each other.

Gandhi's birthday

The birthday of Mohandas Gandhi on 2nd October is now a national holiday throughout India.

Glossary

caste the social status or position into which a Hindu person is born

centenary 100th anniversary

climate the average weather conditions over a long period of time

democracy country run by a government voted into power by the people

dialects languages spoken by people in different regions of a country

dynasty ruling family

economy the way a country uses its money, goods and services

emblem symbol that represents a country

fast not eat anything at all

fertile describes rich soil that can produce lots of fruits and vegetables

festivals when people come together to celebrate an event by eating, drinking and dancing

illuminated manuscript colourful decoration on written paper or printed document

Indian subcontinent India and its neighbouring countries Bangladesh, Pakistan and Sri Lanka

kharma the Hindu belief that a person's past actions may have an effect on his or her present and future status

monsoon season of heavy rains, from June to August

national anthem official song of a country

plateau area of flat land that is higher than the surrounding land

poverty when someone has little or no money or material possessions

prime minister person elected by the people to run a country

prostrate lie flat on the ground

rainforests dense tropical forests with heavy rainfall

rangoli colourful designs made on the floor near the entrance to a house or temple to welcome guests

sacred holy; of religious significance

saffron golden yellow spice that comes from the inside of crocus flowers

Sanskrit ancient literary language used by many Indian writers

saris lengths of cloth wrapped around the body and worn as traditional dress by Indian women and girls

symmetrical able to be divided into two halves that are the same

traditionally a way of doing something that has been passed down through the generations

Find Out More

Books

Das, Prodeepta. *Prita Goes to India*
(Children Return to Their Roots)
Frances Lincoln
ISBN: 978 1 8450 7430 2

Flatt, C. *Facts about Countries India*
Franklin Watts
ISBN: 978 0 7496 6030 7

Ganeri, Anita and Wright, Rachel.
Country Topics India
Franklin Watts
ISBN: 978 0 7496 7330

Festivals of the World: India
Franklin Watts
ISBN: 978 0 7496 6771 9

Hirst, Mike. *Festivals and Food India*
Wayland
ISBN: 978 0 7502 4842 6

Jaffrey, Madhur. *Seasons of Splendour: Tales,
Myths and Legends of India*
Puffin
ISBN: 978 0 1403 4699 2

Websites

www.incredibleindia.org
This is the official site of India's
Department of Tourism and is packed
with information on every aspect of
life in India.

www.bbc.co.uk/history/ancient/india
This useful website explores the ancient
sites that helped to shape the history
and culture of India.

www.historyforkids.org/learn/india
Clear information on India's history.

**www.travel-himalayas.com/himalayan-
mountains-peaks/**
Website packed with information on the
different peaks of the Himalayas,
including Everest.

www.tajmahal.org.uk
This site contains everything you need
to know about the Taj Mahal.

http://timesofindia.indiatimes.com
Visit India's leading newspaper online to
find out about what's happening in India.

Index